BOOK ONE
30 Days of Inspiration for the Woman's Soul

Dew Drops

R. MARTIN

Introduction

Dear sisters in Christ—
May God bless you wherever you serve.
Thanks to all who helped bring this booklet into being.
All honor is the Lord's.
   -R. Martin

"The aged women likewise, that they be...teachers of good things; That they may teach the young women to be sober, to love their husbands, to love their children, To be discreet, chaste, keepers at home, good, obedient to their own husbands, that the word of God be not blasphemed" (Titus 2:3-5).

© Carlisle Press 2014 All Rights Reserved

All rights reserved. No portion of this book may be reproduced by any means, electronic or mechanical, including photocopying, recording, or by any information storage retrieval system, without written permission of the copyright owner, except for the inclusion of brief quotations for a review.

ISBN: 978-1-93375338-6
Rebecca Martin
Book Design by: Lori Troyer
Printed in the USA by Carlisle Printing of Walnut Creek

Carlisle Press
WALNUT CREEK

2673 Township Road 421
Sugarcreek, Ohio 44681

phone | 800.852.4482

Table of Contents

Refresh, Revive, Renew 2
We're Alive–Let's Live Like It 4
An Evil Replacement 6
Empty Shell 8
Thorns and Sin 10
Is It Dependable? 12
Casting Our Cares 14
A Garden of Spices 16
That Ye May Be Able to Stand 18
Light from Within 20
Who Was Being Judged? 22
Never-Ending Stream 24
Grand Finale 26
A Well-Stocked Store 28
Thunder and Tears 30
Jeshurun Waxed Fat 32
Innocent Blood 34
Collops of Fat 36
Beyond Remorse 38
Threshing the Mountain 40
The Lord's Joy 42
Jesus Needs Us 44
Way, Truth, and Life 46
How Can We Glorify God? 48
To Love Is to Obey 50
Like The Lily 52
Like the Cedars 54
Like the Olive Tree 56
The Sweet-Smelling Savor 58
Only from Behind 60

Day 1

Refresh, Revive, Renew

"**Oh Mother, the** flowers are dead!" Little Rhoda ran into the house to gasp out this tragic news. "I wonder if they got too thirsty."

Taking Rhoda's hand, Mother suggested, "Let's go out and have a look at the flowerbed." The petunias, planted in the blazing sun, were certainly a sorry sight. Prostrate on the parched earth they lay, their exhausted petals ugly and shriveled.

"We forgot to water them," Mother said with remorse. "Tonight after the sun goes down, we will bring these flowers plenty of water."

Rhoda asked in surprise, "You mean they are not dead? They can stand up again?"

"Yes, I believe they can," Mother affirmed.

But the evening turned out to be a hectic one, and the flowers were forgotten. The minute she woke up the next morning, Rhoda asked, "Did you water the flowers, Mother?"

Mother clapped a hand to her mouth. "I'm sorry. I forgot."

Rhoda dashed outside. Moments later she skipped back in high glee. "Mother, they're standing up again! Come and see."

"The dew must have revived them," Mother marveled, gazing at the gloriously unfurled petals that only yesterday had seemed near death.

Bible lands were often parched from lack of rain. No wonder the Bible writers used the morning dew as a symbol of revival and renewal.

Have you ever read the prophet Hosea's marvelous portrayal of the repentance and restoration of Israel? It's the last chapter in his book. He begins with a tender call: "O Israel, return unto the Lord thy God; for thou hast fallen by thine iniquity…"

By verse 4 we have the Lord's loving, gracious response. "I will heal their backsliding, I will love them freely…"

Then in verse 5, this beautiful picture of the reviving dew: "I will be as the dew unto Israel: he shall grow as the lily, and cast forth his roots as Lebanon…"

Solomon in Proverbs draws this striking parallel: "The king's wrath is as the roaring of a lion, but his favour is as the dew upon the grass."

Job too, in describing his better days, used the dew as an illustration: "My root was spread out by the waters, and the dew lay all night upon my branch. My glory was fresh in me, and my bow was renewed in my hand" (Job 29:19, 20).

How can sin-parched souls receive God's refreshing, restoring dew? Going back to Hosea 14, the picture is completed: (v.7) "They that dwell under his [the Lord's] shadow shall return; they shall revive as the corn, and grow as the vine." Let us dwell under the shadow of Jehovah's wings and ever wait to receive the refreshing dew of His Word.

Day 2

We're Alive—Let's Live Like It

How blessed the Yoder family felt that evening, to have Daddy back home again. For six days he had lain in the hospital with head injuries after a car accident. Three of those days had been spent in a coma.

"When I saw you there on the bed, I thought you were dead," Jerome confessed, snuggling in Daddy's arms in the easy chair. "You didn't move and you didn't talk, but Mother said you weren't sleeping. So I thought you must not be alive."

Father rubbed his chin on the top of Jerome's curly head. "Well, I was. You might say I was alive—but I didn't know it."

In Hosea 6:1&2, the prophet was referring to God's punishment of Israel at the hands of the Assyrians; but shining through the words is a beautiful portrayal of the Saviour, wounded on the cross, yet rising victorious. "For he hath torn, and he will heal us; he hath smitten, and he will bind us up. After two days will he revive us: in the third day he will raise us up, and we shall live in his sight."

It is very significant that the prophet used the words *we* and *us*. "He will raise *us* up, and *we* shall live." You and I as believers are included! Christ rose, the firstfruits, and we revive with Him.

The apostle says the same in Eph. 2:4-7: "But God, who is rich in mercy, for his great love wherewith he loved us, Even when we were dead in sins, hath quickened us together with Christ (by grace ye are saved); And hath raised us up together, and made us sit together in heavenly places in Christ Jesus."

Amazing words. And it's all in the past tense—final and finished. In the purpose of God the believers have been raised from the grave of sin and are seated with the risen Lord in the place of acceptance and victory. We were one with Christ when He lay in the grave and arose.

The pity is that we too often do not believe this, nor live and act as if we did. By grace we are brought into this position; as Paul goes on to say, we are created in Christ unto good works—let us walk in them!

"For as in Adam all die, even so in Christ shall all be made alive" (1 Cor. 15:22).

As believers, we've been "made alive" in Christ—let's live as if we believed it!

Day 3

An Evil Replacement

"**Oh, I like** Christmas," gloated Sally, hugging herself in delight.

Mother took the opportunity to ask a searching question. "Just what are the things about Christmas that you like so much?"

"Oh, everything," Sally gushed. "The feeling. The anticipation. School programs. Lots of candy. Having all the family at Grandmas' for dinner. Gifts…" The look on Mother's face made Sally pause. Lamely, she added, "And, of course, hearing the Christmas story at church. I guess that's the most important part, really."

"Christ is the most important part," Mother emphasized, while inwardly she wondered, *Are we letting our children substitute earthly pleasures for something that is crucial to the saving of our souls?*

"And he set a graven image of the grove that he had made in the house [temple], of which the Lord said to David, and to Solomon his son, In this house, and in Jerusalem, which I have chosen out of all tribes of Israel, will

I put my name forever" (2 Ki.21:7).

Do you see what is happening in that verse? Idols are being set up right in the temple of God!

"He" is Manasseh, one of the most wicked kings of Judah. Beginning at the age of twelve, he reigned for 55 years, longer than any other of the kings. What terrible abominations he introduced! Forsaking the God-fearing ways of his father, Hezekiah, Manasseh was not content to worship his heathen idols only in the high places he built for them. No, he brought his graven images right into the temple and worshiped them there. Such an evil replacement—filthy idol altars where the holy Altar of Sacrifice was to hold sway.

We would never do such a thing, would we?

Wait. There is much about today's celebration of Christmas that makes us uneasy. We observe a "holiday" that coincides with an ancient pagan festival, claiming to commemorate in snowy December what must have taken place in summer when the flocks were on pasture. We occupy our minds with cards, gifts, shopping, programs, and food. Christmas. The word is not even found in the Scriptures.

The Scriptures speak of God's love for mankind, of a Baby and a lowly birth, of a simple, unworldly Life lived here on earth by the Son of God, and ultimately of the death He died to save us.

Idols in the temple of God? Perhaps it is time to do some honest searching of our hearts.

Day 4

Empty Shell

They had not gone far after leaving a friend's new house before Anna burst out, "I've never seen such grand retirement quarters before!"

Her husband shrugged. "You know I don't notice houses."

"Well, listening to Vera as she toured me through their new home, I realized it had been built for her—down to the last detail. I mean, her every wish was consulted and fulfilled. It appears that John wanted to provide as many conveniences as possible for his wife," Anna rattled on. Then she added quickly, "But I wouldn't trade our own little place for theirs."

Three months later, Vera learned that she had a brain tumor. In another month she passed away. Anna's throat choked up as she entered John and Vera's "grand" house for the viewing. And on the way home, she cried as her husband shared what John had disconsolately said to him: "Without Vera, this house is nothing but an empty shell."

There was once a house so grand that it took seven years to build. Tens of thousands of men were employed to hew stones and transport building materials. More thousands did fine work in cedar and jewels and precious metals. Nothing was spared to make the house as beautiful as possible.

As you may have guessed, this "house" was the temple that Solomon built for the Lord. At last the great day came when all was finished and the ark of the covenant was brought to its resting place in the holy of holies. Along with the priests, Solomon held a great ceremony to dedicate the temple. Was he waiting with a trace of anxiety, wondering whether God would visibly take possession of this new dwelling, as He had the tabernacle of Moses in the wilderness? I'm sure Solomon knew that this great temple would be nothing without the presence of God.

He came! In the Shekinah glory of the cloud, God came—but not until after the priests had gone out of the sanctuary. When the sacrifices had ended and the choir began singing praises, then God filled His house with unspeakable glory.

What of the house that is our life? Unless it is owned by the living God, dwelt in by Him, sanctified by His presence, it is nothing but an empty shell. If we want God in our hearts, all else must come out so that the rightful owner may come in.

He will surely come, if we have offered the sacrifice of a "broken and contrite heart." Once we begin to "praise the name of God with a song, and magnify him with thanksgiving" (Ps.69:30), He will come in His Shekinah glory to take possession of the temple that is our life.

Day 5

Thorns and Sin

Planning an excursion to pick blackberries near the forest, Mother told the children, "Wear your oldest clothes. And if possible, wear something that doesn't tear easily."

"Why?" questioned Cleason, who had not gone blackberrying before.

Mother replied, "Because of the brambles. Blackberry thorns are wicked."

Secretly, Cleason didn't think thorns could be that bad. But he donned a pair of tough, oft-mended trousers and followed his mother and sisters to the blackberry patch.

At first they mostly picked the berries on the perimeter of the patch. Even there, unprotected arms were mercilessly scratched and brambles grabbed at skirts.

The berries in the center of the patch looked so luscious! At last Cleason forged his way in, and was amazed at the clutching, gouging power of those brambles. "Ow!" he yelled. "You'd think these thorns are out to get me."

"I told you they're nasty," Mother reminded him.

And Hannah said quietly as she picked away, "I guess thorns have been around ever since Adam and Eve sinned, haven't they, Mom?"

When you think about it, thorns and sin are closely connected. Thorns came because of sin. "Because thou hast… eaten of the tree, of which I commanded thee, saying, Thou shalt not eat of it: cursed is the ground for thy sake… Thorns and thistles shall it bring forth to thee," God told Adam in Genesis 3.

Is that why Jesus had to wear a crown made of thorns? The thorns of sin were platted together and pressed down over His forehead till the blood ran down His face. "He was wounded for our transgressions, he was bruised for our iniquities: the chastisement of our peace was upon him; and with his stripes we are healed" (Isa.53:5).

Jesus took the thorns of sin upon Himself. God sent Him for that very purpose. "Yet it pleased the Lord to bruise him; he hath put him to grief" (Isa.53:10). Yes, as Isaiah states further, the soul of Jesus became an offering for our sin.

And here is the triumph of that offering, that crown of thorns: "He shall see the travail of his soul, and shall be satisfied" (Isa.53:11). May we be there on that great day when Christ surveys the millions who were saved because of His soul's travail, His crown of thorns. May we be witness of His satisfaction when the crown of thorns is forever cast down and the crown of eternal glory is set upon His brow!

Day 6

Is It Dependable?

November's fluctuating weather brought viruses, coughs, colds. After Father and little Jamie had been coughing for a week, Father declared, "It's time to bring out my mother's cough medicine." Going to the cabinet, he brought out a bottle containing a thick greenish liquid.

"So that's what that is!" exclaimed his wife. "I've noticed that unlabeled bottle in there ever since we're married."

Father grinned as he shook the bottle. "I don't know what my mother all mixed together to make this, but I remember that it used to be effective. You could depend on this stuff to chase a cough."

The lid came off, and Mother drew closer to sniff it. "Whew—what a smell! Are you sure this medicine is still okay to use?"

"I don't see why not," he said defensively. "I remember it always smelled pretty powerful."

"Surely you'll try it yourself before we give any to Jamie," she requested.

"Of course." Bravely, he downed about a tablespoon of the stuff.

In a minute, he was retching and coughing. Within half an hour he had a violent stomachache. He admitted miserably, "The stuff must have gone bad. Guess it's not as dependable as I thought."

"Let your conscience be your guide." There are people who feel they can depend on their own conscience to govern their lives.

Can our conscience be depended on? Is there not a possibility that it will "go bad" and lead us in the wrong direction?

Consider Pilate. At first, confronted with Jesus, the conscience of Pilate was startled. Here was a Man who claimed to be King. Unlike other prisoners Pilate had known, this one did not seem to have any desire to escape.

Next we see Pilate struggling with his conscience. In private, he asked Jesus that greatest of questions: "What is truth?" In public, he offered Barabbas to the people, and when they refused, he asked a very un-judge-like question: "What then shall I do with Jesus?" Pilate was facing the greatest struggle of his life, a struggle between his own deep conviction and the demands of the crowd.

But Pilate compromised his conscience. For the sake of his position, he gave Jesus over to the bloodthirsty crowd.

And in the end, Pilate's conscience was drugged into silence. He washed his hands of the whole affair. Conscience was dead.

A man who runs his life simply by conscience is likely to ruin his life.

DAY 7

Casting Our Cares

"MOTHER, I AM so worried," Emma confided when she came home from school one evening.

Mother looked up from her sewing. "And what are you worried about, my dear?"

Emma flung her school books down on the table. "What if I don't get a passing mark on this history test? And next week we have spelling and arithmetic tests. What if I fail those too? Or the English and geography tests we'll have the week after that? Because if I don't get good marks on the tests, I won't pass into sixth grade!" By the time she had poured out this catalog of woes, Emma was near tears.

"Ah, Emma," said Mother. "Suppose I asked you to fill the wood box. What if I said you have to carry in the whole boxful at once? Would you be able to do that?"

"Why no, Mother," responded Emma. "You know I can take only one armload at a time."

"Of course. And that's how we'll tackle your tests—one at a time. Here, I'll help you study history," Mother proposed.

"I knew you'd make me feel better," Emma beamed.

Mother's heart was also warmed. Her little girl had brought her cares and found comfort.

In reading Luke 21:34, it's startling to realize this: our cares—our worries and anxieties—are considered just as detrimental to salvation as the obvious sin of drunkenness. "Take heed to yourselves, lest at any time your hearts be overcharged with surfeiting, and drunkenness, and cares of this life…"

The same thing shows up in the parable of the sower, in Mark 4:19. Ranked right up there with deceitfulness of riches and other lusts are the cares of this world, choking and smothering the good seed.

Oh, the worries and cares of this world! How fitting that they are compared to thorns. They are so entangling, so vexing and scratching.

Yet Jesus commanded us not to worry. "Take no thought for [do not worry about] your life, what ye shall eat, or what ye shall drink; nor yet for your body, what ye shall put on" (Matt.6:25).

The apostle exhorts the same. "Be careful [anxious] for nothing" (Phil.4:6).

But we women are so prone to be like Martha. It was not without reason that Jesus reprimanded her, saying, "Martha, Martha, thou art careful and troubled about many things" (Luke 10:41).

How can we break free from the trend of worry?

Listen to the rest of Paul's advice in Phil.4:6: "But in everything, by prayer and supplication, with thanksgiving, let your requests be made known unto God."

And Peter has such a clear answer too. "Casting all your care upon him [God], for he careth for you" (1 Pet.5:7).

Day 8

A Garden of Spices

"Mother, when are we going to look at Grandma's garden?" eight-year-old Erma begged.

Reluctant to interrupt the conversation with Grandma, Eva looked down at her daughter. "I didn't know you'd be so eager to see the garden."

"Oh, I can hardly wait!" Erma chirped. "When I was in the yard just now, the wind was blowing and I could smell the garden. It smells *soo* good!"

Still trying to put her off, Eva hedged, "You could just go and have a look on your own."

"But I need you and Grandma to tell me what all the plants are," Erma persisted.

That got Grandma to her feet. "Let's go to the garden before lunch yet. We'll still have a few hours to talk before you go home again."

It was good for Eva to view that garden through Erma's eager eyes. Of course she'd seen it before, but today as Erma bubbled with questions about the different herbs, spices, and perennials, she realized anew what a gardener her mother was. And Erma was right. What an array of sweet aromas was borne on the breeze!

The church of Christ is compared to a garden of spices in Song of Solomon 4:12-14. "A garden enclosed is my sister, my spouse. Thy plants are an orchard of pomegranates, with pleasant fruits; camphire, with spikenard; Spikenard and saffron; calamus and cinnamon, with all trees of frankincense; myrrh and aloes, with all the chief spices."

Then in verse 16, the church prays for the blessed Spirit to make the fragrance flow. "Awake, O north wind; and come, thou south; blow upon my garden, that the spices thereof might flow out."

This prayer was answered in the pouring out of the Spirit on the day of Pentecost: "And suddenly there came a sound from heaven as of a rushing mighty wind" (Acts 2:2).

Thus the church is as a garden of the Lord, enclosed for Him. The blessed Spirit in His operations is as the north and south wind. The north wind is for conviction: "And when he [the Spirit] is come, he will reprove the world of sin, and of righteousness, and of judgment" (Jn.16:8).

The south wind comes gently, as a comforter. "And I will pray the Father, and he shall give you another Comforter, that he may abide with you forever; I will not leave you comfortless: I will come unto you" (Jn.14:16,18).

Do you see, then, how the gales of the Spirit are needed to flow forth the spices of grace? And all this is needed for fruit-bearing, that the church may say to the Bridegroom, "Let my beloved come into his garden, and eat his pleasant fruits" (S.S. 4:16).

Day 9

That Ye May Be Able to Stand

Stricken with rheumatoid arthritis at a young age, Judy was in a wheelchair by the time she reached her teenage years. However, the therapist Judy started seeing when she was 17 would not give up entirely on her mobility. "You should get more of those stiff muscles moving," Tracey told her. "Who knows? Maybe we'll get you walking again."

"Do you really mean that?" Judy asked in disbelief.

"I mean it," came the firm reply. "We'll start by teaching you to stand on your own two feet."

So Judy entered a rigorous regimen of exercise and massage. As the weeks passed, her own courage would have faltered, but Tracey refused to give up. "Let's set a goal," she proposed. "Your sister who teaches school will be home for the Christmas holidays. Wouldn't it be nice if you could surprise her by being able to stand?"

That made Judy's eyes sparkle. Mother and the two other girls spent hours with her therapy, and Tracey came twice a week. What a treat it was to see the oldest sister's face when Judy stood in her presence!

We know that the angels stand before Jehovah's throne. "I am Gabriel, that stand in the presence of God," came the angel's dignified reply when the perplexed Zacharias asked for an affirmation of his amazing tidings.

To think that we too will one day stand in the presence of God! But how can mere humans stand before so great a judge? We are unworthy. John lamented in Rev. 6:17, "For the great day of his wrath is come; and who shall be able to stand?"

If we want to be able to stand on that great day before the Lord, then we must learn to stand here. "Wherefore take unto you the whole armour of God, that ye may be able to withstand in the evil day, and having done all, to stand" (Eph.6:13). So says the apostle, and again in Col. 4:12, "…that ye may stand perfect and complete in all the will of God."

Luke, in 21:34&36, tells us in more detail what we must do to stand. "And take heed to yourselves, lest at any time your hearts be overcharged with surfeiting, and drunkenness, and cares of this life… Watch ye therefore, and pray always, that ye may be accounted worthy…to stand before the Son of man." Watching and praying. That is the only way we can guard against the things that would rob us of our standing.

Day 10

Light from Within

"**Let's go for** a walk in the snow tonight," Mother proposed. "With the moon nearly full, it's very bright outside." So she and the two oldest children helped bundle the younger two into warm wraps, and they set out across the crisp snow. Long blue shadows wavered along beside them. Above, the moonglow spread all across the sky.

"It's almost like daylight," observed Susan.

"The sun is a lot brighter than the moon, though," Aaron pointed out.

Jason, their five-year-old question-box, wondered, "Why? Why does the sun have so much more light than the moon?"

"Well, you see, the moon has no light of its own," Mother explained. "That light you see is only a reflection of the sun's light."

Crunching on through the snow, they all thought that over. After a while Katie mused, "So that means the moon's light is only on the outside, but the sun's light comes from inside."

His time in the presence of God left a glow on the face of Moses. Stephen's face shone too, though he saw the Son of man for only a moment. But in Matthew 17 we see on the face of a Man a light that came from within. "And [he] was transfigured before them; and his face did shine as the sun."

What an experience that must have been for the privileged three who saw Jesus there! For a few glorious minutes they caught a glimpse of that usually hidden Shekinah glory breaking through the veil of the Lord's human flesh. "And we beheld his glory," exclaims John in 1:14, "the glory as of the only begotten of the Father, full of grace and truth."

Yet here is a remarkable thing. You know those familiar words at the beginning of Romans 12: "Be ye transformed by the renewing of your minds." Did you also know that in the Hebrew, the very same word used for "transformed" here, was used for "transfigured" in the account of Christ's glorification?

That means you and I may also be "transfigured" by a light from within. We may do more than momentarily see and reflect our Lord's face. For us, too, it is to be an inner thing. Jesus wants to dwell in our hearts. He wants us to cast off the encumbering veil—to "put off the old man" so His light can shine forth.

Let us not be like those described in 2 Cor. 4:4: "In whom the god of this world hath blinded the minds of them which believe not, lest the light of the glorious gospel of Christ, who is the image of God, should shine unto them."

Rather, may it be with us as Paul says two verses further on: "For God, who commanded the light to shine out of darkness, hath shined in our hearts, to give the light of the knowledge of the glory of God in the face of Jesus Christ."

Day 11

Who Was Being Judged?

MANY YEARS AGO in Antwerp, a young maiden was brought before the judges because of her faith. When the bailiff asked this girl—whose name was Janneken—whether she had been rebaptized, she gave this forthright reply: "Question me in regard to my faith, and I will freely confess it to you; or are *you* ashamed of it?"

The bailiff must have been a bit taken aback. However, he forged on with the verdict: "We've done enough to gain you; it's too bad you didn't recant."

Back came this fearless response: "You have loved my flesh, but not my soul; but God will receive my soul and make it an heir. And though you are now a bailiff in your glory, you will regret it when you come before God's judgment, and wish that you had rather been a herdsman in the fear of God" (*Martyrs Mirror*).

Janneken received the death sentence and was drowned. But as we survey the scene of her trial, we ask ourselves: *Who was really being judged? The bailiff or the believing maiden?*

Jesus declared in John 9:39, "For judgment I am come into this world." And again, in John 12:31, He said, "Now is the judgment of this world: now shall the prince of this world be cast out." He was speaking in a tense we can't comprehend; not past, not present, not future, but the ever-present NOW of eternity. Though Christ's death and resurrection had not yet taken place, in the sight of heaven the world was already judged and the devil was being cast out.

Not so very long after Jesus made these powerful statements, this greatest Judge the world has ever known was brought before a little earthly judge named Pontius Pilate.

Do you think Pilate felt comfortable in the presence of this august Prisoner? It's possible that Pilate began to feel as though he were the prisoner and Jesus the Judge. From this Man emanated the calm serenity of One who knows that the world with all its Pilates is already judged.

Don't we hear a note of ever-increasing perplexity in Pilate's questions? "Art thou the king of the Jews?" he asked, perhaps in scorn at first.

"My kingdom is not of this world," came the unfathomable reply.

Pilate was unnerved. "Art thou a king then?"

"Thou sayest that I am a king," responded Jesus. "For this cause came I into the world, that I should bear witness of the truth."

By this time, Pilate must have been thoroughly uncomfortable. He reacted as a worldly man would: by trying to shrug it off. "What is truth?" he shot back carelessly.

Indeed, what is the truth? Who was being judged?

Day 12

Never-Ending Stream

Evening had come—the time for looking back over the day and seeing a string of failures littering its landscape. "Why can't I be a better mother?" cried Lydia as she prayed for mercy and forgiveness.

Sleep brought refreshment. In the morning Lydia purposed, "Today I will do better. I will not snap at the children when they whine and quarrel. I will chasten them when they need it, and give help when they need it. All day I will be sweet and true and loving, as mothers ought to be."

But alas, her resolutions were like a spring that gushes up in the early morning, only to dry up under the sun's oppressive rays. At night, once again, Lydia looked back and saw where she had failed. Again she cried, "Why can't I be a better mother?"

The Psalmist made resolutions too. In 119:57 he declares, "I have said that I would keep thy words." But bitter experience revealed this fact to the Psalmist: human strength does not avail. "Put not your trust…in the son of man, in whom there is no help… in that very day his thoughts perish"

(Ps.146:3&4). Our own strength is but a failing spring.

What is the remedy? Let's look to those memorable words of Jesus in John 4:14: "The water that I shall give him shall be in him a well of water springing up into everlasting life." And again in John 7:38: "He that believeth on me, as the scripture hath said, out of his belly shall flow rivers of living water."

When we allow Jesus to do His work in our soul, our heart is connected to the reservoirs of eternity! Supplies from God's own heart rise up in our soul.

We may still fail, because our flesh is weak; but when we abide in Him, the sap of His life will renew and reinforce the purposes of the holy life. God waits for us to echo the Psalmist's prayer in 51:10—"Create in me a clean heart, O God; and renew a right [steadfast] spirit within me."

God wants us to be rooted and grounded in Christ (Eph.3:17). Then only can be manifested in us the fruit of the Spirit: "love, joy, peace, longsuffering, gentleness, goodness, faith, meekness, self-control" (Gal.5:22, 23). *Lord, in our weakness we pray for the never-ending stream of Your life flowing through us.*

Day 13

Grand Finale

Because they all had a German heritage, the parents of Elsie's students wanted her to teach several German hymns each school year. Unfortunately, the children were not too enthused. Elsie sometimes felt hard-pressed between the parents' expectations and the children's dislike.

When she did teach a German song, she tried to present it in a manner that piqued their interest. One music period she printed on the blackboard the words GRAND FINALE. "Can someone read this to us?" she requested.

An eighth-grader's hand went up tentatively. "Is that word pronounced the same as 'finally'?"

"Not quite. The word is from the Latin, and you say it fĭn-ăl´-ĭ. It rhymes with Sally. It refers to the concluding portion of a musical composition," Elsie explained. "And if a song has a 'grand finale', it ends with a flourish! Our song today certainly has a grand finale."

She handed out copies of the German song. Immediately one of the seventh-graders wondered, "Is it because each verse ends with two 'Hallelujahs'? Is that the grand finale?"

"Exactly," smiled Elsie. "This is a hymn of such high praise to God that only 'Hallelujahs' could really express the feeling. 'Hallelujah,' you see, is a Hebrew word meaning 'Praise the Lord.'"

So they began to learn the song. What a pleasure, when the earnest young voices pitched in to sing the praises of song number 392 in *Philharmonia!* "Praise the Lord, O my soul! I will praise Him unto death; As long as I can count hours on earth, Will I sing praises to my God… Hallelujah, Hallelujah!"

The world's greatest collection of hymns has a grand finale too. The last five chapters in the book of Psalms—146-150—are known as the "Hallelujah Psalms." It's true that our *KJV* starts each of these chapters with "Praise the Lord"; but if you check the margin, you'll realize that in Hebrew these Psalms began—and some of them ended too—with a rousing "Hallelujah."

What transcendent praise we find in this five-part finale to the Psalms! "Happy is he…whose hope is in the Lord his God," trumpets 146—praise for God's help. 147 overflows with praise for God's providence; it contains not a single complaint or petition. 148 calls to all creation to praise Him. 149 is a shout of praise for triumphant victory in the Lord.

And in Psalm 150, each phrase seems to build upon the preceding one to a grand climax of universal praise. Not merely the priests and Levites, nor merely the congregation, but all the creatures of time and space which breathe are included in this choir of choirs!

There the Psalter ends, but the melody lingers on… "Hallelujah, Hallelujah, Hallelujah!"

(Hint: Song 392 in *Philharmonia* seems to have borrowed most of its points from these five Psalms.)

Day 14

A Well-Stocked Store

"**Mom, the Tilley** light isn't working right!" called Annie from the living room. "It's so dim that I can't see to do my sewing."

Back from the kitchen came Mom's advice, "Pump in some more pressure."

"I already did, and it doesn't help," Annie protested. Still, she pumped away for another few seconds. Nothing changed. The mantle that was supposed to glow brightly cast only a few feeble sputtering rays.

Finally, Dad came to see what was the matter. "Hmm. Doesn't seem to be the mantle that's causing trouble. The next thing that usually causes problems is a little part up in here." He tapped the top of the stainless-steel lantern.

Annie sighed. "If we still lived in Pennsylvania, all we'd have to do is run down the road to Uncle Aaron's and get what we need."

"I don't know of a Tilley dealer in this community. We'll have to write Aaron and ask for parts," Dad decided.

The next forenoon before they got the letter mailed, however, one of their neighbors dropped in. Dad happened to mention the dilemma of the malfunctioning Tilley.

"Oh yes, we have a Tilley dealer here," the neighbor assured him. "David Yoder, over on the edge of town. He'll have anything you need."

Did you know that Romans 15 provides a picture of God's store? We find in that chapter a three-fold description of the "wares" God has available for us at all times.

In verse 5 He is called "the God of patience and consolation."

In verse 13 He is "the God of hope."

And in verse 33 He is "the God of peace."

Patience, consolation, hope, and peace. It is all there in His Word—His store—waiting for us to do as Isaiah invites in 55:1: "Ho, everyone that thirsteth, come ye to the waters, and he that hath no money; come ye, buy and eat; yea, come, buy wine and milk without money and without price."

However, before we'll get around to patronizing God's well-stocked "department store," we must recognize that we need something. And Romans 15 supplies that sense of need, too, in the very first verse: "We that are strong ought to bear the infirmities of the weak." If you're like me, such words certainly induce a feeling of inadequacy. Faced with Paul's injunction to help others and bear their infirmities, we protest, "But we are not strong. We have nothing to offer."

Ah, no—but have we forgotten? We have a Father whose well-stocked warehouse shelves stretch into infinity; a Father who says to all as He said in Luke 15:31—"Son, thou art ever with me, and all that I have is thine."

There is no excuse. In faith we can help ourselves to the Father's wares, then go forth fully equipped to impart them to others around us.

DAY 15

Thunder and Tears

GERALD LOOKED RUEFULLY at Amos and said, "That was quite a lecture, wasn't it?"

Amos shrugged as he led the way to the bike stand. "She wasn't exactly angry, though."

"You don't think so?" exclaimed Gerald, mounting his bike and heading for home. "She certainly was stern. Didn't you see the way her eyes flashed?"

Amos pedaled a short way down the road before replying. "I guess we deserved it," he said finally.

Perhaps if these two seventh-grade boys could have peeked into the classroom just then and seen the person they were discussing, they would have spoken differently. Their teacher sat at her desk, head down on her arms, while sobs heaved her shoulders. Her errant pupils had no idea how easily a schoolteacher's "thunder and lightning" can give way to the rain of tears.

Do we hear only thunder in the woes Jesus pronounced upon the scribes and Pharisees in Matt.23? Certainly He didn't mince words; He condemned them for seven things:

For neither entering the kingdom of heaven themselves, nor allowing others to enter.

For converting people away from God to be like themselves.

For paying attention to details while ignoring the important things: justice, mercy, and faith.

For keeping up appearances when their private life was corrupt.

For acting spiritual to cover up sin.

For pretending to learn from past history, when their conduct showed they had not.

But how quickly the Lord's stern diatribe melts into these tender, yearning words: "O Jerusalem, Jerusalem, how often would I have gathered thy children together, even as a hen gathereth her chickens under her wings, and ye would not!" Such a humble similitude He used—a barnyard hen and her chicks—yet it is the very heart of God expressed.

Christ wants nothing more than to gather poor souls home to Himself. As the Psalmist says in 91:4, "He shall cover thee with his feathers, and under his wings shalt thou trust."

Yet the Jews, His chosen people, refused His loving admonitions. "They would not." No wonder Christ's thundering denunciations of woe gave way to tender tears.

Day 16

Jeshurun Waxed Fat

Breathless with excitement, Annie reported to her mother, "Do you know what? Uncle Joe is coming tomorrow, and we'll hitch up Ranty for the first time."

"Oh." Mother's voice didn't match Annie's enthusiasm. Ranty, you see, was a horse their family had "rescued" a few months ago. When he arrived on their farm he'd been gaunt, unhealthy—and mean. Whatever ill treatment he'd suffered at his former home had turned him into an ill-tempered animal.

However, Annie and her dad were true horse lovers. With the help of Uncle Joe—a true horse trainer—they wrought a transformation in Ranty. His gaunt frame had rounded; he was now the picture of good health as he frisked about the lush pasture.

"Do you really think Ranty has lost his mean streak?" Mother queried, looking down into Annie's flushed face.

"Aw, Mom," she groaned. "We've showered him with love and attention. Why would he want to be mean to us?"

Why, indeed? Why did Annie come to Mother in tears the next day after their attempt at hitching up the new horse? Why did she have to sob out a story of a horse so frisky that he kicked the training cart to smithereens and bolted out of the pasture? It was beyond Annie's comprehension how her beloved horse could have done such a thing.

Have you ever read the song of Moses—the one God bade Moses to speak to Israel before he died? Much could be said about this noble song, found in Deut.32, but we'll concentrate on verse 15: "But Jeshurun waxed fat, and kicked: thou art waxen fat, thou art grown thick, thou art covered with fatness; then he forsook God which made him, and lightly esteemed the Rock of his salvation."

"Jeshurun" has been defined as a pet name for Israel. Moses in his song describes all the blessings God heaped upon His people—and what happened? Once Israel was prosperous and well-fed, they broke from the harness and turned against the Lord.

What folly! Did they not realize how much they depended on the Rock, the fountain of their salvation? They were just like a rebellious horse that runs away from his master, only to discover what a lean life he must lead without that loving care.

We don't need to look away from ourselves. When things are easy—when we forget from whom all these mercies flow—is not rebellion often the next step? Let us not be like "Jeshurun" and "lightly esteem" the Rock of our salvation.

Day 17

Innocent Blood

Munching an after-school snack of peanut butter cookies, Ellen related to her mother, "Sometimes on Fridays we have a story-appreciation period. That's when the teacher reads a short story to us, and then takes marks on how well we answer oral questions. Today's story was pretty tough—"

"Because it was from the *Martyrs Mirror*," broke in Viola. "I'm pretty sure I didn't get good marks. I had a hard time following the story."

Ellen shot her a look that said, *You shouldn't interrupt.* Then she continued, "I had to listen hard too. The story was about these Anabaptists who were taken to court, where the authorities brought different charges against them. And Mother, the strange part was, the charges didn't really sound like they'd done anything bad."

"They sounded more like compliments than complaints," remarked Viola.

Ellen nodded. "The authorities were saying how the Anabaptists don't drink and swear and steal—as if their very honesty could be held against them. I could hardly figure it out, Mother."

"Maybe those authorities had a hard time figuring it out too," Mother responded. "It makes you think of the people who tried to condemn Jesus. Why, Pontius Pilate actually declared, 'I find in him no fault at all.'"

Do you know who gave one of the most compelling testimonies to Christ's innocence? None other than Judas Iscariot. After selling Jesus for thirty pieces of silver—after betraying Him with a false kiss—we find Judas suddenly sick with remorse, flinging those gold pieces at the chief priests' feet and wailing, "I have sinned in that I have betrayed the innocent blood."

By nature, Judas was covetous and thievish. He would not have been inclined to think generously of anyone. Had he seen even one questionable feature in Jesus as he walked with Him those three years, Judas would have remembered it. He would have fastened upon it now to excuse the terrible deed he had done.

But there was nothing—nothing at all—in Christ's sinless life for Judas to fasten upon. Thievish, covetous, and dishonest though he was, Judas could not say one word against Jesus, not even to those who had pronounced Him guilty. From Iscariot's lips could come only this stark confession: "I have betrayed innocent blood."

Ah, sinless, innocent Lamb! Yet your "soul was made an offering for sin," and you have borne "the sins of many" (Isa. 53:10&12). "For he hath made him to be sin for us, who knew no sin; that we might be made the righteousness of God in him" (2 Cor. 5:21).

Dew Drops {ONE}

Day 18

Collops of Fat

Some young ladies were discussing the practice of providing extra serving bowls for dessert at mealtime. One of the girls declared, "To me, those little bowls are nothing but extra work."

"But I don't like to have my first course mixed with my second course on my plate," protested another maiden.

Still another retorted, "All you need is a piece of bread to wipe your plate clean after first course."

Then someone offered the clincher that silenced them all: "I don't suppose starving people even have a second course, let alone spend time arguing about the merits of extra bowls to serve it with."

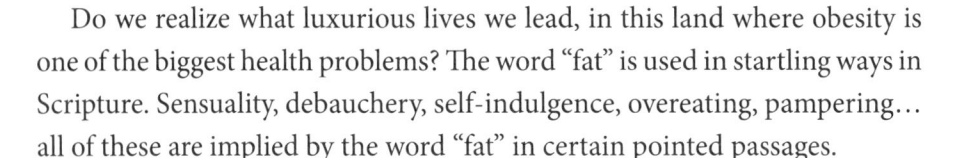

Do we realize what luxurious lives we lead, in this land where obesity is one of the biggest health problems? The word "fat" is used in startling ways in Scripture. Sensuality, debauchery, self-indulgence, overeating, pampering… all of these are implied by the word "fat" in certain pointed passages.

Psalm 73 uses graphic language to describe those with excessive food

Dew Drops {ONE}

and riches. "Their eyes stand out with fatness: they have more than their heart could wish." The marginal translation for "stand out with fatness" says "bulge with abundance." We get the picture!

On to Psalm 17:10 for another description of licentious living. "They are inclosed in their own fat." The marginal translation is even more vivid: "have closed up their fat hearts."

And then in Job 15:27, a rich oppressor is described thus: "Because he covereth his face with his fatness, and maketh collops of fat on his flanks." Whew!

The most sobering part is the dreadful outcome of such self-indulgence. In each of the passages we get the same picture: sensuality results in rebellion against God and against God's people. Psalm 17 says, "with their mouth they speak proudly" (against God). It goes on to compare the "fat" ones to a "lion that is greedy of his prey" (v.12). In Psalm 73 we are told that the "fat" ones "set their mouth against the heavens" (v.8&9).

And what a terrible thing is said of the "fat" one in Job 15! "He stretcheth out his hand against God, and strengtheneth himself against the Almighty."

Yet here is the sad final verdict for the one who "fattens" himself with worldly goods: "He dwelleth in desolate cities, and in houses… which are ready to become heaps… neither shall his substance continue…" (Job 15:28-29).

Day 19

Beyond Remorse

"I wish you could tell me what I should do about my cousin Leah," Ruth said to her husband one evening.

Adam's expression was blank. "Leah? Why would you need to do anything about her?"

"Remember the rumor that circulated a few weeks ago? It was completely false, and nasty too," Ruth reminded him.

"Oh, you mean about our apples. But what has Leah got to do with that?" Adam still seemed puzzled.

"Because she feels it was her fault that the rumor started," explained Ruth. "The problem is Leah's remorse. It's excessive, I'd say. Every time she sees me she gets tears in her eyes and starts apologizing all over again."

Adam nodded sympathetically. "It would be nice if she could just be thankful that the rumor is cleared up now. Too much remorse can be as bad as none at all if you cling to it and let it destroy your happiness."

The Jews may have been nearly overwhelmed with remorse, that day in the newly rebuilt city of Jerusalem when Ezra read to them from God's law. For many years during the Babylonian captivity, God's law had been neglected. Now as the people stood from morning until noon on the street while Ezra read to them, they realized the enormity of their sin. "All the people wept, when they heard the words of the law" (Neh.8:9).

But Ezra and the Levites would not let the people wallow in their remorse. "This day is holy unto the Lord," they remonstrated. "Mourn not, nor weep… Go your way, eat the fat, and drink the sweet, and send portions unto them for whom nothing is prepared," they cried to the weeping crowd.

At this, the people did a complete about-face. Whereas in verse 9 they had all been weeping, in verse 12 we find them feasting and laughing. And why? "Because they had understood the words that were declared unto them" (Neh.8:12).

When once we really understand God's Word, it is a perpetual feast to us. Yes, at first it convicts us of sin, and we are overcome with remorse when we realize what sinners we are. But let us not stop there. Unrestrained remorse will only weaken us. The Lord wants us to go on in joy—the joy of sin forgiven and hope renewed, a joy so abundant that it overflows as we "send portions unto them for whom nothing is prepared."

DAY 20

Threshing the Mountain

AT LAST THE great work had begun. All summer the children had noticed the sign at the end of the road: CONSTRUCTION TO BEGIN AUG. 25. Now the huge yellow machines were moving in. Clattering noises echoed through the valley as iron teeth began chewing at the hillside. Soon truckloads of crushed rock were roaring down the curve to be deposited at the bottom of the slope.

"I still can't believe it that they're going to lower our hill," remarked Jerry, his nose pressed against the window to watch the machines.

Lucy marveled, "It'll be so much easier for the horses to get up here."

"Safer, too," Jeremy reminded her. "That sharp turn at the bottom of such a steep hill was a bad spot."

By summer's end, the job was complete. Where formerly the road had climbed steeply, there was now a gentle grade. Where it had turned a sharp corner, there was now a sweeping curve. "They did it!" exulted Jeremy. "They moved our mountain."

Dew Drops {ONE}

Is there a mountain in our life that seems impossible to climb? We need to remember that passage in the book of Isaiah where God promises Israel that they shall thresh mountains. "Fear not, thou worm Jacob, and ye men of Israel… Behold, I will make thee a new sharp threshing instrument having teeth: thou shalt thresh the mountains, and beat them small, and shalt make the hills as chaff. Thou shalt fan them, and the wind shall carry them away, and the whirlwind shall scatter them: and thou shalt rejoice in the Lord, and shalt glory in the Holy One of Israel" (Isa. 41:14-16).

Our problems shall be thoroughly dealt with! They will completely disappear, blown away as chaff on the wind! But how can this come to pass?

The key lies in the word "worm." We must realize that we are as nothing—nothing more than a puny worm trying to burrow into that mountain. Did you know that even Jesus is called a worm by the Psalmist? Check it out in Psalm 22, which is a description of our Lord laying down His life on the cross. Jesus tasted the dregs—yes, even to the extent of becoming a "worm"—yet God raised Him to glorious heights of power.

So let us not fret about that huge mountain in front of us. We have the promise: though in ourselves we are no better than worms, we shall "rejoice in the Lord, and glory in the Holy One of Israel."

Day 21

The Lord's Joy

Sometimes when she came home on a Sunday afternoon, Laura was exhausted. There had been Sunday evenings when she simply fell into bed and her husband had to prepare supper.

Tonight was different. Laura still felt vigorous after a full day of church and visiting. "Let's cook macaroni for supper," she proposed to little Joanna.

"Oh, goody," cried the five-year-old.

"And we could heat up some wieners too," Laura planned.

Joanna began skipping around the table. Soon the two-year-old and the four-year-old were hopping after her. When Daddy came inside, he was amazed to find his three daughters circling the table and singing, "I'm so happy, so happy, happy, happy!"

Grinning, he inquired, "And what makes our girls so happy tonight?"

Over at the stove, Laura paused in her stirring and mixing. What would Joanna reply? Would she attribute her happiness to the macaroni and wieners?

Joanna stopped skipping. Face beaming, she explained to Daddy, "I'm happy because Mother's happy."

In Nehemiah 8:10 we find these words: "For the joy of the Lord is your strength." What brings joy to our God? Are we told enough about the heart of the Lord that we can fathom what causes Him to rejoice?

Let's look at a few verses that may give us a glimpse.

First, Hebrews 12:2. There we see the joy that the Lord has in redeeming His people.

Next, in Zeph.3:17 we find the joy He has in possessing us, His inheritance. Amazing words, considering how unworthy we are: "The Lord thy God… will rejoice over thee with joy; he will rest in his love, he will joy over thee with singing."

And third, in John 15 we find Jesus speaking of the joy it brings Him to indwell us for fruit-bearing.

Now we as Christians do have a joy of our own. We rejoice in the Lord, and in all that He has done for us. But let's face it, our joy tends to fluctuate due to our feebleness.

That is why the Lord's joy is best of all. His joy in ransoming us—in indwelling us to bear fruit—and in possessing us as His bride—is our real strength. Our joy in Him may be a changeable thing: His joy in us knows no change. "These things have I spoken unto you," said Jesus in Jn.15:11, "that my joy may remain in you, and that your joy might be full."

Day 22

Jesus Needs Us

"I HOPE I can play in the grape arbor today," bubbled Mary, on the seat beside her mother. The two were on their way to Grandpas', where Mary always enjoyed playing house beneath the climbing grapevines. After greeting her grandparents, Mary was soon dressing up the dolls and carrying them to the arbor.

Minutes later she came back inside. Sadly she said, "Mother, the grapevine doesn't have branches anymore. Something must have eaten them up."

"No, Mary, nothing ate them. Grandpa pruned the branches on purpose," Grandma explained.

Mary looked bewildered. "Why would he do that? The vine can't have grapes if there are no branches."

"Grandpa didn't cut them all off," Grandma corrected her. "Come out to the arbor, and I'll show you."

So Mary followed her to the arbor, which did look very bare, compared to last summer's leafy proliferation. "See, here is a branch, and here, and here," Grandma pointed out. "Grandpa left only the best parts. It was high time to prune the vines, Mary. And do you know what? Next summer there

Dew Drops {ONE}

will be better grapes than ever!"

The vine needs the branches in order to bear fruit. "I am the vine, ye are the branches," Jesus says in Jn.15:5. Jesus needs us.

Without us He cannot bless men as He would. Isn't that a sublime thought?

Jesus needs something that I can yield Him! He needs me to bear fruit in the world, to be as Joseph was: "a fruitful bough, whose branches run over the wall" (Gen.49:22).

Jesus may need us, but we need Him even more. "Without me ye can do nothing," he said (Jn.15:5). Service to God and man is possible only through abiding union with Him.

Nor can we bear fruit without God's pruning and purging. "Every branch that beareth fruit, he purgeth it, that it may bring forth more fruit" (Jn.15:2). Let us yield ourselves to be pruned by the Word. "Now ye are clean [purged] through the word which I have spoken unto you" (Jn.15:3). How many of our own promptings and ideas must be "cut off" in order that the best fruit may be yielded!

Day 23

Way, Truth, and Life

A LONG FIVE-HOUR wait stretched in front of us. We slumped in the bus terminal seats, dreading boredom, yet having no idea where we'd want to go to pass the time in this city.

Before long a small, wiry man sat down near us and struck up a conversation. Not many minutes passed before we realized what his passionate interest was: raising non-hybrid grains for heritage seeds. Having similar interests ourselves, we had no lack of things to talk about.

"You should come and see my fields," the man urged. "I'm only two miles out of town, up in the hills. Follow me and I'll show you the way to my place."

We explained, "We have no vehicle."

He jumped up, exclaiming without hesitation, "Then I'll take you there myself."

"I am the way, the truth, and the life." Few words of Christ's are more familiar to us. Let's examine the three claims separately.

I am the way. "No man cometh unto the Father, but my me," Jesus declares in the same verse. Through sin, we were barred forever from the tree of life. But Jesus provided another way, through His death and resurrection. In Him, man and God are brought together.

I am the truth. Jesus is the reality of all that we find in the Father when we get there, because "in him dwelleth all the fullness of the Godhead bodily" (Col.2:9). That is why, as Paul points out in Eph.4:20&21, we want to "learn Christ"—we want to hear Him—we want to be taught by Him, and grasp the "truth [that] is in Jesus."

I am the life. At the end of his first epistle, John yearns, "That we may know him that is true, and we are in him that is true, even in his Son Jesus Christ. This is the true God, and eternal life" (1 Jn.5:20). We are "alive unto God [only] through Jesus Christ our Lord" (Rom.6:11).

Yes, Jesus is the way, the truth, and the life—the beginning, the middle, and the end. But really, the three cannot be separated. They flow together, as in these words from Hebrews 10:20: Jesus is the true and "living way." Truth and life are not only at the end, but all along the way. For even if we knew the way and the truth, we would not in ourselves have the strength and life to get there. Jesus, and Jesus alone, is the way to the Father; He is the truth that directs us to the way; and He is the life that animates us upon the way.

Day 24

How Can We Glorify God?

CATHEDRAL-LIKE, THE TREE branches met in graceful arches far above. Except for birdsong and the wind sighing in the leaves, silence reigned in the great forest. The three women hiking the pine-needle-cushioned trail felt almost compelled to walk on tiptoe in the awesome stillness. When they spoke, it was in hushed tones.

Their steps quickened as the sun dropped lower. Though they had not taken this trail before, others had told them what to expect at the end, and they were full of anticipation.

Just as the sunset unfurled its banners of rose and magenta, the three hikers arrived at the forest's edge. Below, the land fell away in a steep cliff, and beyond lay a vast forested valley stretching to the flaming horizon.

In their thirty-something years of life, these three women had hiked many a trail. They knew it was a privilege not so freely available to their married friends, so they made the most of each opportunity to glorify God for His creation.

Today was no exception. Sitting on the edge of that cliff, the three sang hymn after hymn of praise as the sunset flared then faded over the darkening valley.

Praise glorifies God. "Oh that men would praise the Lord for his goodness, and for his wonderful works to the children of men! And let them offer the sacrifices of thanksgiving, and declare his works with rejoicing" (Ps.107:21&22).

But God desires more than the "fruit of our lips" for His glorification. When Jesus was upbraiding the Pharisees in Matt.15, He quoted words from Isaiah: "This people draweth nigh unto me with their mouth, and honoureth me with their lips; but their heart is far from me."

How is God most truly glorified? In Psalm 50, the poet reveals to Israel the startling fact that God didn't really need all their sacrifices. Then in verses 14&15 he comes right out and states plainly how we can glorify God. "Offer unto God thanksgiving, and pay [fulfill] thy vows unto the most High: And call upon me in the day of trouble: I will deliver thee, and thou shalt glorify me."

God's greatest glory doesn't come from having infinite tribute paid to Him for His majesty. He is most glorified when we can say, "Lord, I was lost, and You found me; I was a poor blind wanderer in the wilderness, and You came after me and saved me."

Though we may also offer to God the bouquets of His universe, let's remember what glorifies Him most: when we live so as to show others that we owe all to the Lord.

Day 25

To Love Is to Obey

ADA DIDN'T ALWAYS work at school on Saturdays, but on this sunny Saturday in December she decided to take the three-mile drive and get a few things caught up. She had barely tied her horse in the stable at school when she noticed another buggy driving in. To her surprise it was Wilma, a friend of hers who had only started teaching this year. It was certainly going to be interesting to hear how things were going for her.

By the time Ada had the stove going and the classroom warmed up, the two friends were deep in conversation. All too soon, Ada realized that Wilma was burdened. Things were not going as well as Wilma had hoped.

"It's a question of obedience, as far as I can see," Wilma said. "Are those boys simply not taught to obey? All the punishments I've dealt out—all my stern speeches—don't seem to make a difference. What am I doing wrong?"

Ada's heart ached for her friend. But what to say? Gropingly, she offered some advice gleaned from her own nine years of teaching. But when Wilma left half an hour later, Ada did not feel that she had given much help.

Throughout the day, Ada kept pondering their conversation.

Why were her own students so cheerfully obedient? Ada came to a very humbling conclusion: the obedience she saw in her classroom was born out of love.

In the Bible, love and true obedience are inseparable. With stark simplicity Jesus said, "If ye love me, keep my commandments" (Jn.14:15). In his letters John states it even more strongly: "For this is the love of God, that we keep his commandments."

Notice the sequence. First love, then obedience. God does not say, "Keep my commandments, then love me." Pure streams can only come from a cleansed fountain.

Nor does He say, "Keep my commandments, and love me at the same time," as if they were two separate things.

No, love is put first. It is first in importance and first in experience. We must begin with love, and continue by keeping His commandments. Love is the only mother that true obedience can have.

The essence of obedience lies in the love that prompts the deed, rather than in the deed itself. It might be possible to keep Christ's commandments outwardly without being acceptable to God. As long as we would disobey if we dared, then our hearts are not right with God.

In short, to love Christ is to live Christ. Love is no mere weak sentimentality. It is a strong, vigorous response to the motions of the divine love. "If ye keep my commandments, ye shall abide in my love; even as I have kept my Father's commandments, and abide in his love," said Jesus in Jn.15:10.

Day 26

GROWING IN GRACE 1

Like The Lily

LITTLE DORIS WAS fascinated by the scaly bulbs Mother brought home from a neighbor. "Are they something to eat?" she wondered. "They don't look very good."

"No, these are lily bulbs," Mother replied. "You know those beautiful flowers Jacobs have in front of their house? They grow from these bulbs."

Doris took one of the dry, peeling bulbs and rolled it around in her hand. "Such nice flowers from such an ugly thing," she marveled. "Where will we plant them?"

"Come. I'll show you." Mother took the spade and led Doris to the back of the house. "It's a funny thing," she said as she began digging holes. "When these bulbs grow roots, they are liable to come out at the top. Lilies have very shallow roots."

In the last chapter of his book, the prophet Hosea makes us think of a painter who ransacks the world of nature for colours to complete his picture. Throughout his book he often laments the downfall of Israel; but chapter 14 blazes forth with the light of restoration and redemption. Hosea may have been speaking of Israel, but in his writings today we see a prophetic description of the redeemed church, growing in grace.

Lilies are the first illustration Hosea adds to his palette. He has God promising, 'I will be as the dew unto Israel: he shall grow as the lily…' (Hos.14:5)

Such an apt picture of the new birth! Hidden in the ground all winter, the lily-bulbs began to sprout when they receive the early rains of spring. How quickly the stem is formed, and the flower blossoms! So the believers, receiving the reviving showers of grace, spring from the grave of sin to be clothed in the new white garments of the redeemed.

The Song of Solomon also uses the lilies to picture Christ and the church. 'My beloved is gone down into the garden, to the beds of spices, to feed [his flock] in the gardens, and to gather lilies. I am my beloved's, and my beloved is mine: he feedeth [his flock] among the lilies.' (S.S.6:2&3)

Do you see the picture too? Jesus is in the midst of the church, tenderly feeding the lily-white-clad throng of the redeemed.

Yes, lilies resurrect from ugly bulbs and wear gorgeous robes. But they do not have deep roots, so Hosea goes on to find another illustration to describe the church…

Day 27

GROWING IN GRACE 2

Like the Cedars

How the wind roared that night! Edna awoke shivering. She hadn't known the house could make so much noise. The windows rattled and loose shingles flapped in the wind. So strong were the gusts that the house shuddered under the onslaught.

"What if it's a tornado?" asked a small voice from the other bed.

"Oh, I think it's okay," Edna replied, more bravely than she felt.

Her little sister wasn't comforted. "I wish we'd go down to Mother."

Before Edna could say anything, they heard a loud CRASH!

"Let's go," Edna said through chattering teeth. Grabbing their housecoats, the girls fled downstairs. Father and Mother were in the kitchen already. As Father reached for the yardlight switch, Edna watched through the window. "The big tree!" she gasped. "It's down!"

Grotesque with broken branches and bare roots poking at the dark sky, the old soft maple lay prostrate in the yard. "Just look at how shallow those roots were," Father commented. "It's a wonder the tree stayed standing this long."

Next, Hosea adds cedars to his palette. At least that is what we infer as we read on, "…He shall grow as the lily and cast forth his roots as Lebanon. His branches shall spread…" Quite likely he was thinking of Lebanon's cedars, those mighty trees of which the Psalmist spoke in 92:12&13. "The righteous shall flourish like the palm tree: he shall grow like a cedar in Lebanon. Those that be planted in the house of the Lord shall flourish in the courts of our God."

Well might Hosea say that cedars "cast forth" their roots. We have heard that the cedars of Lebanon sent down root systems as deep as the trees were tall! Should not our "growing in grace" also consist most in the roots, deep down out of sight, in the heart? Paul declares, "Though our outward man perish, yet the inward man is renewed day by day" (2 Cor. 4:16).

And where should we be rooted? According to Eph. 3:17, we may be "rooted and grounded in love." In Col. 1:23 Paul tells us to "continue in the faith grounded and settled." And in Col. 2:7 we find the most wonderful place of all for our roots: "Rooted and built up in him"—Christ Himself!

Rooted in Him, we depend on Him for nourishment. The more sap we draw from Him, the more we will grow. "The trees of the Lord are full of sap, the cedars of Lebanon, which he hath planted," declares the Psalmist in 104:16.

Yes, the church needs roots like the cedar. But cedars bear no fruit, so the prophet carries us on to still another comparison.

Day 28

GROWING IN GRACE 3

Like the Olive Tree

"**Tonight at the** gathering," Mother told the children, "you might get to see your new teacher, Rufus Miller. I'm told he's in the area already, doing some work at the school."

"How will we know which man is Rufus?" Robert wondered.

"Well, he's shorter than most men—only a little over five feet tall," Mother told him. "Rufus taught my cousin's children for 15 years, and they really liked him for a teacher."

At the neighborhood gathering, Robert kept his eyes open. Sure enough, he soon spotted a shorter-than-average man in the group. Robert swallowed hard. So this was the nice teacher Mother had spoken of! Rufus had gray hair and thick glasses, and he was anything but handsome.

Time, however, proved Mother right. Just as in the first community he served, Rufus became a beloved, trusted teacher, looked up to by parents and children alike.

"…His branches shall spread, and his beauty shall be as the olive tree…" Hosea continues.

Olive trees? Beautiful? we might ask. We've seen pictures of the olive groves so familiar when Jesus lived in Palestine. The trees have gnarled, grotesque trunks. The branches are insignificant, and the leaves are harsh in texture. Some trees are beautiful for their symmetry, but not so the olive. It is just a twisted, misshapen tangle of trunk and branches. We have to think of the words Isaiah used to describe the Saviour: "For he shall grow up before him as a tender plant, and as a root out of a dry ground: he hath no form nor comeliness; and when we shall see him, there is no beauty that we should desire him" (53:2).

If the olive tree is so unhandsome, why then does Hosea speak of its beauty? Two reasons. For one thing, it is ever green. The Psalmist sings in 52:8, "But I am like a green olive tree in the house of God: I trust in the mercy of God for ever and ever." Eternal life! That is what the olive tree signifies because of its evergreen leaves.

But most of all, the olive tree's beauty lies in its fruitfulness. What does it matter if the trunk is gnarled and the leaves are ugly? Fruitfulness is what the Lord desires. "Herein is my Father glorified, that ye bear much fruit," Jesus said in Jn.15:8.

God causes the believers to grow like the lily, send forth roots like a cedar, bear fruit like the olive tree… But Hosea goes on to mention one more attribute of the church.

DAY 29

GROWING IN GRACE 4

The Sweet-Smelling Savor

THE SETTING IS thousands of years ago, when the Mosaic law was still a new institution and Aaron and his sons were ministering in the wilderness tabernacle. Reuel is an imaginary 12-year-old boy who gets the chance to accompany his father to the tabernacle.

Before they leave, Reuel has many questions for his parents. "Why are we going to kill and burn this lamb?"

"God wants us to bring a burnt offering to atone for our sins," his father explains. "When I put my hand on the head of the offering, God accepts it as an atonement for my sin."

Reuel persists, "But couldn't we offer the lamb some other way? Why must it be burned up?"

"God wants our offering to be wholly consumed," answers his mother. "As Moses told us, this is a sweet savor to God."

So Reuel goes with his father and watches the priests perform the rituals of killing the lamb. Soon an odorous smoke rises as the lamb is consumed.

Walking back to the tent with his father, Reuel admits, "I thought the smell was awful. How can it be a sweet savor to God?"

His father thinks for a long time before answering. "Remember, God is not like us men. Regardless how bad it smells to us, the odor of flesh being offered up must be sweet to Him."

As he concludes his expressive description of the church, Hosea brings smell into the picture. "…and his beauty shall be as the olive tree, and his smell as Lebanon." The prophet may have had in mind the groves of Lebanon, where the air is perfumed with fragrant cedars and flowers.

The "sweet savor" God desires from us is somewhat different from the fragrance of cedar. Already in Genesis we find that God is honored when Noah offers burnt offerings. "And the Lord smelled a sweet savor" (Gen.8:21). Later, God gave to Moses a law that allowed people to atone for their sins through the "sweet savor" of ritualistic burnt offerings.

Christ is the fulfillment of these offerings. The apostle states it so clearly in Eph.5:2: "…as Christ also hath loved us, and hath given himself for us an offering and a sacrifice to God for a sweet-smelling savor."

In Song of Solomon 1:3, the church says of Christ, her lover: "Because of the savour of thy good ointments thy name is as ointment poured forth." By faith in the name of Jesus we partake of His all-sufficient, sweet-smelling sacrifice.

Yes, that is still our part. In faith we lay our hand on the Sacrificial Lamb to identify with Him. In faith we "present our bodies a living sacrifice, holy, acceptable unto God" (Rom.12:1). Only then, as we lay down our lives in complete surrender to Him, can it be as Paul says in 2 Cor.2:15, "For we are unto God a sweet savor of Christ."

Dew Drops {ONE}

Day 30

Only from Behind

"**Today in art** class," announced teacher Sarah, "each of you will draw a picture of the person who sits in front of you."

The expression on her students' faces ranged from astonishment to consternation. Never before had their teacher asked them to draw portraits! A fifth-grader's hand went up. "I can't draw people."

"I'm not asking you to draw whole people," Sarah assured them. "All I want you to do is look at the head and shoulders of the person in front of you, then draw exactly what you see. From the back."

Relief showed on some of the faces. Then came the inevitable question from a person at the front of a row. "But there's no one in front of me to draw!"

Sarah smiled. "After art comes grammar. While the rest of you are drawing, those at the front of the rows will do grammar. Then, while the rest do grammar, those four will sit at the back of the room and draw those persons."

That brought smiles all around. Then Sarah added an interesting requirement: "Don't sign your names to the drawings. We're going to try and guess who each portrait is."

Only from behind. That was the glimpse God granted to Moses when he pleaded, "I beseech thee, shew me thy glory."

"Thou canst not see my face: for there shall no man see me, and live," came God's reply (Ex.33:20). Yet He offered a response to His servant's request. 'I will make all my goodness pass before thee, and I will proclaim the name of the Lord before thee… I will cover thee with my hand while I pass by: And I will take away mine hand, and thou shalt see my back parts: but my face shall not be seen" (Ex.33:19, 22&23).

What an amazing privilege Moses had! What an intimate relationship he must have had with God, even to dare to make such a request.

Yet in a sense we today are even more privileged. True, the New Testament writers also proclaim, "No man hath seen God at any time" (1 Jn.4:12).

But we have Jesus. John says in Jn.1:18, "No man hath seen God at any time; [but] the only begotten Son, which is in the bosom of the Father, he hath declared him." Paul says of Christ that He "is the image of the invisible God" (Col.1:15).

Wonderful truth—we can see the light of God in Christ. Jesus promised those who keep His commandments, "I will love him, and will manifest myself to him" (Jn.14:21).

"For God, who commanded the light to shine out of darkness, hath shined in our hearts, to give the light of the knowledge of the glory of God in the face of Jesus Christ" (2 Cor.4:6).

Then let us be like Moses, of whom the Hebrews writer says in 11:27: "…he endured, as seeing him who is invisible."